THOUGHTS IN A LIBRARY.

BY HENRY M. BAILEY,

LIBRARIAN OF THE YOUNG MEN'S INSTITUTE,

HARTFORD, CONN.

HARTFORD:

F. A. BROWN.

1852.

PRESS OF
CASE, TIFFANY & CO.,
HARTFORD.

Gloria in Excelsis Deo!

TO THE

FREE EPISCOPAL MISSION CHURCH, IN THIS CITY,

WILL BE GIVEN THE MONEY RECEIVED FOR THESE THOUGHTS,

AN OFFERING, IN REMEMBRANCE OF

Elizabeth Bennett and Amos S. Post,

Who, while on earth, walked in the footsteps of the

SAVIOUR.

LIBRARY, *January* 12*th*, 1852.

The Library.

It is a stormy evening: the rain patters on the roof and beats against the windows. All without is cold and cheerless: all within is pleasant and cheerful. The gas burns brightly, and an air of comfort is diffused over everything, in striking contrast to the dreariness of the night without. The table is crowded with readers, and just now there is a momentary stillness: a hush, so deep, that nothing is heard but the ticking of the Library clock, as it measures off the fleeting time. I look around me and think, what a blessing are these books! Here are the works of the mighty dead: thoughts which inspire us now, though they who breathed them have long since turned to dust. Here are treasures which, received into the soul, the "moth and rust cannot corrupt." How beautifully has the wise man said, the "ways of wisdom are pleasantness and all her paths peace." Happy is the young man who lives to cultivate his soul, for within him is a hidden spring of joy which will increase as the light of mind brightens, until he rises to the glories of the eternal world, to "shine as the stars forever and forever."

Books are friends who never desert us. Is the world cold? Here is a retreat where the mind can revel in beauty and sweetness. Here the cares of life can be forgotten for a time, and the soul find rest in communing with genius which is for all time.

How books remind us of the dead! This well worn volume, rich in songs, was the last book read by one whose light footstep was often heard here. She faded away in her bright youth, and through long hours of weariness and pain, found comfort and solace in her favorite authors.

This little book, with turned down leaves, was returned by a father after the funeral of his only child. With what hesitation did he give it up! what a fond, lingering look rested upon it! Dust is upon the brow of his angel boy, and his sweet eyes are closed forever; but those simple pages recall the hours when he played around the household hearth. Again he is seated upon his knee, and he hears again the prattle of his infant voice.

And thou, blest friend, called away in early manhood, this precious book which we read together, brings thee back from the spirit world. I see thee again in the old, familiar place, and watch the soul shining in thy face, as flame illumes an alabaster vase.

But the evening has worn away, the readers are gone, the deep-toned Center bell strikes ten, and it is time to close the Library.

Experience.

Six years within these alcoves. Withdrawn from the tumult of the great world, yet not living in vain, for in those years three hundred thousand volumes have been through these hands.

The boys of the summer of '45, have emerged from round jackets into their first sacks; and have given up Robinson Crusoe and the Lives of the Pirates, and have taken to Hawker on Shooting and the Wandering Jew, who sometimes come back fragrant with the perfume of a mild cigar and "Lubin's double extracts." The laughing schoolgirls who were so eager for Mary Howitt's stories, have become young ladies, and read

Willis' Poems, and think "the Wide, Wide World is perfectly beautiful."

The young gentleman in his first sack is now in the Reading Room, deep in the Merchants' Magazine, but his eyes frequently wander over the cover towards the Librarian's table, where a young lady is waiting for a book. The young lady after some difficulty is suited, and on leaving, happens to look over to the young gentleman, who, by the merest accident, raises his eyes at the same time. The young lady hurries away, and as the door closes after her, the young gentleman comes forward, and with a slight hesitation in his manner, says "He does not wish to be inquisitive, but he would like to know the name of that very pretty young lady who has just gone down stairs!"

O happy spring-time of life, when the dawn of young love first rises in the soul! Let them enjoy the years which can be but once in a lifetime. Let them have them to look back upon, when the romance of life has been pressed out by its realities.

Occasionally, a young member, who has had a serious conversation with a respected friend on light reading, comes to the Library with a face which looks as if the cares of state troubled the mind, and presents a list of historical works, which it would take at least two years to finish; and almost always Rollin's Ancient History heads the paper. We would advise our young friends (and we speak from experience) not to begin when they make good resolutions so fiercely, for disgust is apt soon to follow. We have an edition of the excellent historian Rollin, in eight volumes. But, O "tell it not in Gath!" the first volume has been rebound twice, and the other seven are still quite fresh!

Among the frequenters of the Library there is a little maiden who has just begun to take short flights from home alone. Ever and anon little feet come up the stairs, and a young face presents itself with a timid air. Her soft hair, smoothed by loving hands, looks as if a sunbeam was hid in it, and on her fair brow rests the white dove of innocence. Her eyes, which are "homes of silent prayer," are riveted upon the catalogue; but at length she ventures to call off a number, and is amazed to see a huge black-lettered folio make its appearance. You have pity on her and hand down a book which has never failed to please, in which there is a picture of a little girl with a basket of flowers, playing beside a brook. This is "just the thing." Joy sparkles in the dark blue eyes, and two dimples suddenly appear in cheeks which have become the color of the peach blossom, while the small, rosy mouth reveals a row of little pearls. "Happy Annie!" The school bell rings and she trips away; and as she passes along the street many a care-worn heart blesses her, and loving eyes beam upon her with tenderness. Her father, immersed in the carking cares of business, from the window of his counting-house sees her coming, and his eyes become moist as he lifts his thoughts upward to her mother in Paradise, and wishes that she might have lived to have seen this sweet bud unfold. But she all unheeding passes by, her mind engaged with pleasant fancies, and looking as if an angel walked by her side with folded wings, to shield her from harm. May all good angels guard her.

The Angel's Song.

NIGHT veiled Judea's hills, and on their grassy slopes the shepherds watched their flocks, gently leading those who walked with their young at their side, and carrying the tender lambs in their arms.

The night was calm and beautiful. The starry host gemmed the sky, and not a cloud floated in the blue depths of ether. Midnight passed, and morning drew on apace, when suddenly upon the ears of the watchful shepherds, there fell a strain of heavenly music; and looking up with wonder, lo! a multitude of the angelic host filled the sky, "praising GOD and saying: Glory be to GOD on high, and on earth, peace, good will towards men."

The night was calm and beautiful. Not a leaf rustled in the forests, and the cattle upon a thousand hills stood still. It was as if the great heart of nature had almost ceased to beat. For He has come, the long promised one whom "prophets and kings" desired to see: not as a conqueror, in triumph, but all meek and lowly, "lying in a manger." Sorrow-stricken sons and daughters of poverty and toil, "Lift up your hearts." Wherever you are, for you this Saviour is born. For you the angelic song has been sung. He comes to be a Father to the fatherless, a Friend to the widow, a Guide to youth, a Staff to the aged, and to "suffer the little children to come unto him."

Prisoner, sad and lonely in your solitary cell this night; the iron bedstead let down, and the coarse supper untasted before you; your thoughts busy with the past; your soul all dark with the stains of unrepented sin; your mind harrowed with the remembrance of those whose "gray hairs" you "brought down with sorrow to the grave:" prisoner, lift up your eyes. Behold the star which proclaims the Saviour's coming. Its soft beams fall upon the grated window of your cell, and the shadows take the form of the cross upon the hard stone floor. Prisoner, look at that cross. For you He was lifted up, and while the tide of life beats, there is yet hope for mercy. Behold, He stands at the door and knocks. Throughout the vast prison the slumbering echoes waken. The prisoners all hear Him knocking, and tremble: each guilty heart quakes with fear. Again He knocks: and all fearful the trembling keeper unbars the massive doors, and the glory of His presence illumines the dark corridors. O prisoners! if you will only receive Him, He will come in unto you, and will not reproach you with your old sins, but will simply say, "go and sin no more."

Saturday Evening.

The shades of evening gather upon the hills and brood in the valleys. The laborer turns his weary footsteps homeward, and feels his cares grow lighter as he sees the light in his cottage home, which tells him his cheerful wife waits for him the evening meal. The moon rises and fringes the dark forest trees with silver, and throws a broad beam of light over the placid lake. The dew distils upon the closing flowers, and the cricket chirps in the grass, calling up deep and solemn thoughts of past years. The chimes of distant bells float on the breeze like angel voices, and the old "ivy-mantled tower" casts a shadow upon the monuments in the church-yard, where a pensive mourner treads the ground, rough with graves, and lays an offering of fresh flowers upon a sunken mound.

It is an hour for reflection. A time to think of the blessedness of the day of holy rest approaching. Precious thought! Christ hath arisen. Proclaim it from highest mountain peaks; from the lofty Andes, and from the towering summit of Mont Blanc; and let the isles of the sea catch the joyful sound that Christ hath arisen. In these evening hours he comes to us, and with a voice of heavenly sweetness, says, "Peace be unto you." From that serene brow, once pierced by thorns, a glory emanates which can dispel the thickest clouds of doubt and fear. Thou upon whom the shadow of the angel of death has fallen, and who seest him approaching in the dim distance, lean upon Him who died for us, while passing through that valley in which all the varied paths of life must at last end. Shrink not, gentle spirit: we would go with thee, but thou must go alone; yet not alone, for He hath said, "I will be with thee." The dark waters shall not cover thee.

Could we unseen pass through the homes of the crowded city this night, what pleasant gatherings we might view around the social board. The careless gayety of childhood, the blooming beauty of early womanhood, the pensive sweetness of chastened sorrow, and the pride of manhood, gazing upon home treasures.

Generous youth, leaving for the first time the parental home, to find a place and a name in the thronging marts of commerce: remember her who kneels three times a day in her chamber, with uplifted hands towards heaven, that you may be saved from evil. In the hour of strong temptation, when you tremble at the thought of taking the first step in the broad downward way, resist not the soft touch upon your shoulder, turn not from the mysterious hand upon the wall. It is the counsels of your mother which make you hesitate.

The days of darkness from which none can escape, will come sooner or later to you. The breast from which undying love now springs for you, will be cold in death; and as you look for the last time on the loved form, prepared for the grave, if you can then recall well done duties, her pure spirit will be near you, felt though unseen, and the remembrance of her love will be to you "music at midnight."

The Lord's Day.

How beautifully behind the western hills, sinks the departing sun. This day, in high cathedrals, in simple village churches, and where "two or three" have been gathered together, Christ has been in the midst.

What would life be without this blessed day and all its hallowed associations. To appreciate it, one must have been confined to the chamber of sickness, and on a still summer morning, have listened to the bells, calling the worshipers to the house of prayer. Raised up by the hand of affection and supported by pillows, to think of the pleasant groups wending their way to His holy temples, who "remembereth that we are but dust," and who will guide our feet in the way of peace."

This day through lofty arches has rolled the swelling anthem, and from sweet organs touched by skillful fingers, have arose those heavenly strains which call forth all beautiful and sorrowful emotions, bringing back the dead, blending life's lessons, and lifting up the soul to high communion with its Creator.

We linger in the silent church. The voice of the preacher has died away, and through the rich windows stream the last beams of the setting sun, lighting up for a moment hill and valley, and gilding the spire, which "with silent finger points to heaven."

Remembrance.

They are gone. The autumn leaves have fallen on their graves, and the storms of winter have covered them with a snowy mantle. Spring will return and clothe the earth with beauty, but they will return to us no more.

When the evening bells of the city toll the hour of prayer, and friend meets friend with smiles, our thoughts often rest upon those graves, among the beautiful hills far away. But let us not think of them in the dark grave: they are not there; they have gone to meet the Saviour, to join the innumerable throng who rejoice before God.

"We weep,
But they have done with tears."

Evening Hymn.

Tune, "Spanish Air."

Saviour, in yon world of glory,
  Ever children of thy care,
Low our souls we bow before thee:
  Hear, O hear! our humble prayer.

Angel spirits now are winging
  Through the air their unseen flight,
Peace and joy to mortals bringing,
  In the dark and silent night.

Stars of night are softly beaming
  O'er us from the fount of love:
Rays of heavenly light are streaming
  From the brighter worlds above.

Here around our altar bending,
  Father, unto Thee we come:
Voices low are sweetly blending:
  Father, hear us from thy throne.

www.ingramcontent.com/pod-product-compliance
Lightning Source LLC
LaVergne TN
LVHW011140110826
845150LV00008B/2422

* 9 7 8 1 4 1 8 1 9 3 2 4 9 *